Marx Joyce Abbott Hardy Montaigne Machiavelli Chesterton Cooper Emerson Austen Defoe Melville Haggard Hugo Christie Carroll Eliot Grimm Stoker Molière Wilde Maupassant Byron Schiller Engels Garnett Einstein Fitzgerald Smith Goethe Hawthorne Kafka Cotton Dostoyevsky Hall Baum Kipling Doyle Willis Leslie Dumas Henry Nietzsche Flaubert Turgenev Balzac Stockton Vatsyayana Crane Burroughs Verne Curtis Tocqueville Whitman Gogol Vinci Homer Widger Tolstoy Busch Darwin Thoreau Potter Freud Zola Twain Plato Scott Lawrence Kant Jowett Stevenson Dickens Andersen Burton Hesse Harte London Descartes Cervantes Voltaire Poe Aristotle Wells Hale James Hastings Cooke Bunner Shakespeare Richter Chambers Irving Doré Cicero da Chekhov Benedict Alcott Swift Dante Shaw Wodehouse Pushkin Newton tredition®

tredition was established in 2006 by Sandra Latusseck and Soenke Schulz. Based in Hamburg, Germany, tredition offers publishing solutions to authors and publishing houses, combined with worldwide distribution of printed and digital book content. tredition is uniquely positioned to enable authors and publishing houses to create books on their own terms and without conventional manufacturing risks.

For more information please visit: www.tredition.com

TREDITION CLASSICS

This book is part of the TREDITION CLASSICS series. The creators of this series are united by passion for literature and driven by the intention of making all public domain books available in printed format again - worldwide. Most TREDITION CLASSICS titles have been out of print and off the bookstore shelves for decades. At tredition we believe that a great book never goes out of style and that its value is eternal. Several mostly non-profit literature projects provide content to tredition. To support their good work, tredition donates a portion of the proceeds from each sold copy. As a reader of a TREDITION CLASSICS book, you support our mission to save many of the amazing works of world literature from oblivion. See all available books at www.tredition.com.

Project Gutenberg

The content for this book has been graciously provided by Project Gutenberg. Project Gutenberg is a non-profit organization founded by Michael Hart in 1971 at the University of Illinois. The mission of Project Gutenberg is simple: To encourage the creation and distribution of eBooks. Project Gutenberg is the first and largest collection of public domain eBooks.

Umbrellas and Their History

William Sangster

Imprint

This book is part of TREDITION CLASSICS

Author: William Sangster
Cover design: Buchgut, Berlin – Germany

Publisher: tredition GmbH, Hamburg - Germany
ISBN: 978-3-8424-6395-0

www.tredition.com
www.tredition.de

UMBRELLAS AND THEIR HISTORY

BY

WILLIAM SANGSTER.

"Munimen ad imbres."

CONTENTS.

CHAPTER I.

INTRODUCTORY.

Can it be possibly believed, by the present eminently practical generation, that a busy people like the English, whose diversified occupations so continually expose them to the chances and changes of a proverbially fickle sky, had ever been ignorant of the blessings bestowed on them by that dearest and truest friend in need and in deed, the UMBRELLA? Can you, gentle reader, for instance, realise to yourself the idea of a man not possessing such a convenience for rainy weather?

Why so much unmerited ridicule should be poured upon the head (or handle) of the devoted Umbrella, it is hard to say. What is there comic in an Umbrella? Plain, useful, and unpretending, if any of man's inventions ever deserved sincere regard, the Umbrella is, we maintain, that invention. Only a few years back those who carried Umbrellas were held to be legitimate butts. They were old togies, careful of their health, and so on; but now-a-days we are wiser. Everybody has his Umbrella. It is both cheaper and better made than of old; who, then, so poor he cannot afford one? To see a man going out in the rain umbrella-less excites as much mirth as ever did the sight of those who first—wiser than their generation—availed themselves of this now universal shelter. Yet still a touch of the amusing clings to the "Gamp," as it is sarcastically called. 'What says Douglas Jerrold on the subject? "There are three things that no man but a fool lends, or, having lent, is not in the most helpless state of mental crassitude if he ever hopes to get back again. These three things, my son, are—BOOKS, UMBRELLAS, and MONEY! I believe a certain fiction of the law assumes a remedy to the borrower; but I know of no case in which any man, being sufficiently dastard to gibbet his reputation as plaintiff in such a suit, ever fairly succeeded against the wholesome prejudices of society. Umbrellas may be 'hedged about' by cobweb statutes; I will not swear it is not so; there may exist laws that make such things property; but sure I am that the hissing contempt, the loud-mouthed indignation of all civilised society, 'would sibilate and roar at the bloodless poltroon who should engage law on his side to obtain for him the restitution of a—lent Umbrella!"

Strange to say, it is a fact, melancholy enough, but for all that too true, that our forefathers, scarce seventy years agone, meekly endured the pelting of the pitiless storm without that protection vouchsafed to their descendants by a kind fate and talented inventors. The fact is, the Umbrella forms one of the numerous conveniences of life which seem indispensable to the present generation, because just so long a time has passed since their introduction, that the contrivances which, in some certain degree, previously supplied their place, have passed into oblivion.

We feel the convenience we possess, without being always aware of the gradations which intervened between it and the complete inconvenience of being continually unsheltered from the rain, without any kind friend from whom to seek the protection so ardently desired.

Fortunately a very simple process will enable the reader to realise the fact in its full extent; he need only walk about in a pelting shower for some hours without an Umbrella, or when the weight of a cloak would be insupportable, and at the same time remember that seventy years ago a luxury he can now purchase in almost every street, was within the reach of but very few, while omnibuses and cabs were unknown.

But, apart from considerations of comfort, we may safely claim very much higher qualities as appertaining to the Umbrella. We may even reckon it among the causes that have contributed to lengthen the average of human life, and hold it a most effective agent in the great increase which took place in the population of England between the years 1750 and 1850 as compared with the previous century. The Registrar-General, in his census-report, forgot to mention this fact, but there appears to us not the slightest doubt that the introduction of the Umbrella at the latter part of the former, and commencement of the present century, must have greatly conduced to the improvement of the public health, by preserving the bearer from the various and numerous diseases superinduced by exposure to rain.

But perhaps we are a little harsh on our worthy ancestors; they may have possessed some species of protection from the rain on which they prided themselves as much as we do on our Umbrellas, and regarded the new-fangled invention (as they no doubt termed it) as something exceedingly absurd, coxcombical, and unnecessary; while we, who are in possession of so many life-comforts of which those of the good old times were supremely ignorant—among these we give the Umbrella brevet rank—can afford to smile at such ebullitions as we have come across in those books of the day we have consulted, and to which we shall presently have an opportunity of referring.

We can happily estimate the value of such a friend as the Umbrella, the silent companion of our walks abroad, a companion incomparably superior to those slimy waterproof abominations so urgently recommended to us, for, at the least, the Umbrella cannot be accused of injuring, the health as *they* have been, as it appears, with very good reason. In fact, so long as the climate of England remains as it is, so long will Umbrellas hold their ground in public esteem, and we do not believe that the clerk of the weather will allow himself to be bribed into any alteration, at least for trade considerations.

Another remarkable proof of the utility of the Umbrella may be found in the universality of its use. It has asserted its sway from Indus to the Pole, and is to be met with in every possible variety, from the Napoleon blue silk of the London exquisite, to the coarse red or green cotton of the Turkish rayah. Throughout the Continent it forms the peaceful armament of the peasant, and no more curious sight can be imagined than the wide, uncovered market-place of some quaint old German town during a heavy shower, when every industrial covers himself or herself with the aegis of a portable tent, and a bright array of brass ferrules and canopies of all conceivable hues which cotton can be made to assume, without losing its one quality of "fast colour," flash on the spectator's vision.

The advantages of the Umbrella being thus recognised, it must be confessed that it has hitherto been treated in a most ungrateful and step-motherly fashion. We fly to the Umbrella when the sky is overcast—it affords us shelter in the hour of need—and the service is forgotten as soon as the necessity is relieved. We make abominable jokes upon the Umbrella; we borrow it without compunction from any confiding friend, though with the full intention of never returning it—in fact, it has often been a matter of surprise to us that any one ever does buy an Umbrella, for where can the old Umbrellas go to? Although that question has often been asked concerning the fate of pins, the fact as regards the former, looking at their size, is more curious—and yet, for all that, we treat it with shameful neglect, as if ashamed of a crime we have committed and anxious to conceal the evidences of our guilt.

Let us then strive to afford such reparation as in our power lies, by giving a slight description of THE UMBRELLA AND ITS HISTORY, making up for any deficiencies of our pen by the assistance of the artist's pencil.

CHAPTER II.

THE ANCIENT HISTORY OF THE UMBRELLA.

The Umbrella is derived from a stately family, that of the Parasol, the legitimate use of the Umbrella, though sufficiently obvious, being almost ignored in those countries whence it derives its being, since it was as a protection against the scorching heat of the sun that it was first used. The Parasol, then, or Umbrella—since for all practical purposes the two are really identical—dates from the earliest ages, some commentators on the Bible fancying they can discover it in places where a shade protecting from the sun is mentioned. This is not unlikely, but it is certain that the Parasol has been in use from a very early period.

Chinese history goes a very long way back, inasmuch as it places the invention of these elegant machines many thousand years anterior to the Mosaic date of the world's creation. Their antiquity among the Hindoos is more satisfactorily proved by the following passage from the dramatic poem of *S'akuntâla*, the date of which is supposed to be the 6th century of the Christian era:—

("The cares of supporting the nation harass the sovereign, while he is cheered with a view of the people's welfare, as a huge Umbrella, of which a man bears the staff in his own hand, fatigues while it shades him. The sovereign, like a branching tree, bears on his head the scorching sunbeams, while the broad shade allays the fever of those who seek shelter under him.")

The origin of the Parasol is wrapped in considerable obscurity. Some profound investigators have supposed that large leaves tied to the branching extremities of a bough suggested the first idea of the invention. Others assert that the idea was probably derived from the tent, which remains in form unaltered to the present day. Dr. Morrison, *however*, tells us that the tradition existing in China is, that the *San*, which signifies a shade for sun and rain, originated in standards and banners waving in the air. As this is a case in which we may quote the line—"Who shall decide when doctors disagree?"—we may with safety assume that all are in the right, and that the Parasol owed its origin to all or any of the above-mentioned fortuitous circumstances.

In the Ninevite sculptures the Umbrella or Parasol appears frequently. Layard gives a picture of a bas-relief representing a king in his chariot, with an attendant holding an Umbrella over his head. It has a curtain hanging down behind, but is otherwise exactly like those in use at the present time, the stretchers and sliding runner being plainly represented. To quote the words of that indefatigable traveller:—

"The Umbrella or Parasol, the emblem of royalty so universally accepted by eastern nations, was generally carried over the king in time of peace, and sometimes even in time of war. In shape it resembled, very closely, those in common use; but it is always open in the sculptures. It was edged with tassels, and was usually ornamented at the top by a flower or some other ornament. On the later bas-reliefs, a long piece of embroidered linen or silk falling from one side like a curtain, appears to screen the king completely from the sun. The parasol was reserved exclusively for the monarch, and is never represented as borne over any other person."

In Egypt again, the Parasol is found in various shapes. In some instances it is depicted as a *flabellum,* a fan of palm-leaves or coloured feathers fixed on a long handle, resembling those now carried behind the Pope in processions. Sir Gardner Wilkinson, in his work on Egypt, has, an engraving of an Ethiopian princess travelling through Upper Egypt in a chariot; a kind of Umbrella fastened to a stout pole rises in the centre, bearing a close affinity to what are now termed chaise Umbrellas. To judge from Wilkinson's account, the Umbrella was generally used throughout Egypt, partly as a mark of distinction, but more on account of its useful than its ornamental qualities.

The same author is rather doubtful whether, in the picture given by him of a military chief in his chariot, the frame which an attendant holds up behind the rider is a shield or a screen, but the latter is the more probable supposition, as it has all the appearance of an Umbrella without the usual handle. In some paintings on a temple wall, an Umbrella is held over the figure of a god carried in procession, and altogether we may, perhaps, consider it decided, beyond dispute, that the Umbrella in its modern shape was used in Egypt. [Footnote: To silence captious critics, who may find fault with the designs of our artist, we may once for all remark that an idealised conception of the figures only is given. The style of the ancient draughtsmen was by no means so perfect that we, who live in a more civilised age, should be entirely fettered by their conceptions, and the records of ancient life are not nearly full enough to justify any one who may Assert that the pictures in our pages are not as accurate as those in the British Museum. Anyhow, what they ought to have been, rather than what the ancient were, our artist has striven to delineate.]

In Persia the Parasol is repeatedly found in the carved work of Persepolis, and Sir John Malcolm has an article on the subject in his "History of Persia." In some sculptures—of a very Egyptian character, by the way—the figure of a king appears attended by a slave, who carries over his head an Umbrella, with stretchers and runner complete. In other sculptures on the rock at Takht-i-Bostan, supposed to be not less than twelve centuries old, a deer-hunt is represented, at which a king looks on, seated on a horse, and having an Umbrella borne over his head by an attendant.

This combination of business and comfort forcibly reminds us of a certain wet day in Carlsruhe, where we witnessed from the window of the Hôtel d'Angleterre a stout, martial-looking national guardsman marching to the exercising-ground with an Umbrella over his head, and a maid-servant diligently tramping through the mud behind him, bearing his musket.

As in Assyria, so in most other Eastern countries, this use of the Parasol carried with it a peculiar and honourable significance. The tradition relating to its origin in China has been already alluded to, and we can trace notices of its use a very long way back indeed.

According to Dr. Morrison, Umbrellas and Parasols are referred to in books printed about A.D. 300, but their use has been traced still further back than this. A very ancient book of Chinese ceremonies, called "Tcheou-Li, or The Rites of Tcheou," directs that upon the imperial cars the dais should be placed. "The figure of this dais contained in the Chinese edition of Tcheou-Li, and the particular description of it given in the explanatory commentary of Lin-hi-ye, both identify it with an Umbrella. The latter describes the dais to be composed of 28 arcs, which are equivalent to the whalebone ribs of the modern instrument, and the staff supporting the covering to consist of two parts, the upper being a rod 3/18ths of a Chinese foot in circumference, and the lower a tube 6/10ths in circumference, into which the upper half is capable of sliding."

In the second Tartar invasion of China the emperor's son was taken prisoner by the Tartar chief, and made to carry his Umbrella when he went out hunting.

Starting from the royal significance attached to the Umbrella, came a feeling of veneration for it, very different from the contempt with which we are now-a-days too apt to regard it. It was represented by many ancient nations as shading their gods. In the Hindoo mythology Vishnu is said to have paid a visit to the infernal regions with his Umbrella over his head. One would think that in few places could an Umbrella have been less appropriate, but doubtless Vishnu knew what he was about, and had his own reasons for carrying his *Parapluie* under his arm. Perhaps like Mrs. Gamp he could not be separated from it. So much for the ancient history of our subject in the East. We may now go on to countries about which we know a little more than of ancient China and Assyria.

In Greece, as Becker tells us in his "Charicles," the Parasol was an indispensable adjunct to a lady of fashion. It had also its religious signification. In the Scirophoria, the feast of Athene Sciras, a white Parasol was borne by the priestesses of the goddess from the Acropolis to the Phalerus. In the feasts of Dionysius (in that at Alea in Arcadia, where he was exposed under an Umbrella, and elsewhere) the Umbrella was used, and in an old has-relief the same god is represented as descending ad *inferos* with a small Umbrella in his hand, like Vishnu before mentioned.

There was also another festival in which they appeared, though without any mystical signification. In the Panathenæa, the daughters of the Metceci, or foreign residents, carried Parasols over the heads of Athenian women as a mark of inferiority,

"tas parthenons ton metoikon skiadaephorein en tais rompais aenankazon."
—*OElian, V. H.*, vi. 1.
[Footnote: "They compelled the maidens of the Metceci to act as umbrella-bearers in the processions."]

Its use seems to have been confined to women. In Pausanias there is a description of a tomb near Pharæ, a Greek city. On the tomb was the figure of a woman—

"themapaina de autae prosestaeke skiadeion pherousa." —*Pausanias*, lib. vii., cap. 22, Section 6. [Footnote: "And by her stood a female slave, bearing a parasol."]

Aristophanes seems to mention it among the common articles of female use—

"aemin men gar son eti kai nun tantion, o kanon, oi kalathiokoi, to skiadeion." —*Aristophanes, Thesmoph.*, 821. [Footnote: "For now our loom is safe, our weaving-beam, our baskets and umbrella."]

It occurs frequently on vases, and is in shape like that now used.
It could be put up and down.

"ta d' ota g'an son, nae AL', exepetannuto osper skiadeion, kai palin xunaegeto." —*Arist. Eq.*, 1347. [Footnote: "But your ears, by Jove, are stretched out like a parasol, and now again shut up."]

Which the Scholiast explains, *ekteinetai de kai systelletai pros ton katepeigonta kairon.* [Footnote: "Are opened and shut as need requires."] For a man to carry one was considered a mark of effeminacy, as appears from the following fragment of Anacreon:—

"skiadiskaen elephantinaen phorei gunaixin autos."
Athenaeus, lib. xii., cap. 46, Section 534.
[Footnote: "He carries an ivory parasol, as women do."]

Plutarch makes Aristides speak of Xerxes as sitting under a canopy or Umbrella looking at the sea-fight—

"kathaeenos hupd skiadi chrysae."
Plut. Therm., c. 16 (p. 120),
[Footnote: "Sitting under a golden canopy."]

and of Cleopatra in like manner—

"upo skiadi chrysopasto."
Plut. Anton., c. 26 (p. 927).
[Footnote: "Under a gold-wrought canopy."]

From Greece it is probable that the use of the Parasol passed to Rome, where it seems to have been commonly used by women, while it was the custom even for effeminate men to defend themselves from the heat by means of the *Umbraculum,* formed of skin or leather, and capable of being lowered at will. We find frequent reference to the Umbrella in the Roman Classics, and it appears that it was, not unlikely, a post of honour among maid-servants to bear it over their mistresses. Allusions to it are tolerably frequent in the poets. Virgil's "Munimen ad imbres" [Footnote: "A shelter for the shower."] probably has nothing to do with Umbrellas, but more definite mention of them is not wanting. Ovid speaks of Hercules carrying the Parasol of Omphale:—

"Aurea pellebant rapidos umbracula soles, Quæ tamen Herculeæ sustinuere manus." —*Ov. Fast.,* lib. ii., 1. 31 I. [Footnote: "A golden umbrella warded off the keen sun, which even the hands of Hercules have borne."]

Martial speaks of a servant carrying the Parasol:—

"Umbellam lusca, Lygde feras Dominæ." —*Mart.,* lib. xi., ch. 73. [Footnote: "Mayst thou, Lygde, be parasol-carrier for a publind mistress."]

Juvenal mentions an Umbrella as a present:—

"En cui tu viridem umbellam cui succina mittas"
—*Juv.,* ix., 50.
[Footnote: "See to whom it is sent a green umbrella and amber

ornaments"]

Ovid advises a lover to make himself agreeable by holding his mistress's Parasol: —

"Ipse tene distenta suis umbracula virgis" *Ov. Ars.* Am., ii., 209. [Footnote: "Yourself hold up the umbrella spread out by its rods"]

This shows that the Umbrella was of much the same construction as ours.

A very common use for it was in the theatre, whenever, from wind or other cause, the *velarium* or huge awning stretched over the building (always open to the air) could not be put up: —

"Accipe quæ nimios vincant umbracula soles, Sit licet, et ventus, te tua vela tegont." —*Mart.,* lib. xiv., Ep. 28. [Footnote: "Take this, which may shield you from the sun's excessive rays. So may your own sail shield you, even should the breeze blow."]

By *tua vela* is to be understood "your own Umbrella." And elsewhere the same writer gives the advice: —

"Ingrediare viam coelo licet usque sereno
Ad subitas nunquam scortea desit aquas."
—Man'., lib. xiv. Ep. 130.
[Footnote: "Though with a bright sky you begin your journey, let this cloak ever be at hand in case of unexpected showers."]

It will be noticed from the above extracts that the Umbrella does not appear to have been used among the Romans as a defence from rain; and this is curious enough, for we know that the theatres were protected by the *velarium* or awning, which was drawn across the arena whenever a sudden shower came on; strange that this self-evident application of the Umbrella should not have occurred to a nation generally so ingenious in the invention of every possible luxury. Possibly the expense bestowed in the decoration of the *umbraculum* was a reason for its not being applied to what we cannot but regard as its legitimate use.

After the founding of Constantinople, the custom of great people carrying an Umbrella seems to have arisen, but in Rome it appears only to have been used as a luxury, never as a mark of distinction, Pliny speaks of Umbrellas made of palm-leaves, but from other sources we may gather that the Romans—at all events in the days of the empire—lavished as much splendour on their Umbrella as on all the articles of their dress. Ovid (as above quoted) speaks of an Umbrella inwrought with gold, and Claudian in the same way has:—

"Neu defensura calorem Aurea submoveant rapidos umbracula soles." —*Claud.*, lib. viii., De. iv. cons. Honorii, 1. 340. [Footnote: "Nor. to protect you from the heat, let the golden umbrella ward off the keen sun's rays."]

From this we may conclude that the carrying an Umbrella was in some sort a mark of effeminacy. In another place carrying the Umbrella is alluded to as one of the duties of a slave:—

"Jam non umbracula tollunt
Virginibus," etc.
[Footnote: "*Now* they do not carry girls' parasols."]

Gorius says that the Umbrella came to Rome from the Etruscans, and certainly it appears not infrequently on Etruscan vases, as also on later gems. One gem, figured by Pacudius, shows an Umbrella with a bent handle, sloping backwards. Strabo describes a sort of screen or Umbrella worn by Spanish women, but this is not like a modern Umbrella.

Very many curious facts are connected with the use of the Umbrella throughout the East, where it was nearly everywhere one of the insignia of royalty, or at least of high rank.

M. de la Loubère, who was Envoy Extraordinary from the French King to the King of Siam in 1687 and 1688, wrote an account entitled a "New Historical Relation of the Kingdom of Siam," which was translated in 1693 into English. According to his account the use of the Umbrella was granted to some only of the subjects by the king. An Umbrella with several circles, as if two or three umbrellas were fastened on the same stick, was permitted to the king alone, the nobles carried a single Umbrella with painted cloths hanging from it. The Talapoins (who seem to have been a sort of Siamese monks) had Umbrellas made of a palm-leaf cut and folded, so that the stem formed a handle. The same writer describes the audience-chamber of the King of Siam. In his quaint old French, he says:—"Pour tout meuble il n'y a que trois para-sol, un devant la fenêtre, a neuf ronds, & deux à sept ronds aux deux côtéz de la fenêtre. Le para-sol est en ce Pais-la, ce que le Dais est en celui-ci."

Tavernier, in his "Voyage to the East," says that on each side of the Mogul's throne were two Umbrellas, and also describes the hall of the King of Ava as decorated with an Umbrella. The Mahratta princes, who reigned at Poonah and Sattara, had the title of Ch'hatra-pati, "Lord of the Umbrella." Ch'hatra or cháta has been suggested as the derivation of *satrapaes* (*exatrapaes* in Theopompus), and it seems a probable derivation enough. The cháta of the Indian and Burmese princes is large and heavy, and requires a special attendant, who has a regular position in the royal household. In Ava it seems to have been part of the king's title, that he was "King of the white elephant, and Lord of the twenty-four Umbrellas." Persons of rank in the Mahratta court, who were not permitted the right of carrying an Umbrella, used a screen, a flat vertical disc called AA'-ab-gir, carried by an attendant. Even now the Umbrella has not lost its emblematic meaning. In 1855 the King of Burmah directed a letter to the Marquis of Dalhousie in which he styles himself "His great, glorious, and most excellent Majesty, who reigns over the kingdoms of Thunaparanta, Tampadipa, and all the great Umbrella-wearing chiefs of the Eastern countries," &c.

Thus we see that the same signification which was attached to the Umbrella by the ancient people of Nineveh, still remains connected with it even in our own time.

In the Great Exhibition of 1851 was the splendid Umbrella belonging to his Highness the Maharajah of Najpoor. The ribs and stretchers, sixteen in number, divided the Umbrella into as many segments, covered with silk, exquisitely embroidered with gold and silver ornaments. The upper part of the design was complete in each department, but at the lower, it was formed into a graceful running border, to which a fringe was attached. The handle was hollow and formed of thick silver plates.

In Bengal it appears that no distinction is attached to the Umbrella, since the poorer classes there use a cháta or small Umbrella, made of leaves of the *Licerata peltata*. These are of conical form and have numerous ribs and stretchers. The higher class in Assam use a similar Umbrella.

In China the use of the Umbrella does not appear to have been confined, as in India and Persia, to royalty; but it was always, as it is now, a mark of high rank, though not exclusively so. There seems to have been no particular rule about it, but it carried with it some peculiar distinction; for, on one occasion at least, we hear of twenty-four Umbrellas being carried before the Emperor when he went out hunting. Here it is, what it appears to be in no other Eastern country, a defence against rain rather than sun, and while the richer people do not go out much while it is wet, the poorer classes wear a dress that protects them from the weather. In the rainy season, for instance, a Chinese boatman wears a coat of straw, and a hat of straw and bamboo. Such a dress, of course, renders an Umbrella superfluous, and it matters little to the wearer how hard the rain may pelt. Nevertheless great numbers of Umbrellas are exported from China to India, the Indian Archipelago, and even South America. In the 1851 Exhibition two only were shown. Of them the report says, "They present nothing remarkable beyond the great number of ribs, which amount to forty-two. The ribs are formed of wood; and instead of being embraced by the fork of the stretcher, as in the case of European Umbrellas, they have a groove cut out in the middle of their lengths, into which the stretcher is secured by a stud of wood. The head of each rib fits into a notch formed in the ring of wood, which is fastened on to the top of the stick, there being a separate, notch for each rib. The slide is of wood, and has forty-two notches, namely, one for each stretcher, which like the ribs, is formed of wood. The covering of the Umbrellas exhibited is of oiled paper coarsely painted."

But the use of the Umbrella travelled westward, and with it the custom of regarding it as a mark of dignity.

Amongst the Arabs the Umbrella was a mark of distinction. Niebuhr, who travelled in Southern Arabia, describes a procession of the Iman of Sanah. In it the Iman and each of the princes of his numerous family, caused a *madalla,* or large Umbrella, to be carried by his side; and it is a privilege which, in this country, is appropriated to princes of the blood, just as the Sultan of Constantinople permits none but his vizier to have his caique, or gondola, covered behind, to keep him from the heat of the sun. The same writer goes on to say that many independent chiefs of Yemen carried *madallas* as a mark of their independence.

In Morocco, according to a passage quoted by a writer in the *Penny Magazine* from the Travels of Ali Bey, the emperor alone and his family are allowed to use it. "The retinue of the Sultan was composed of a troop of from fifteen to twenty men on horseback. About a hundred steps behind them came the Sultan, who was mounted on a mule with an officer bearing his Umbrella, who rode by his side also on a mule. The Umbrella is a distinguishing sign of the sovereign of Morocco. Nobody but himself, his sons, or his brothers dare to make use of it." In Turkey the Umbrella is common. A vestige of the reverence once attached to it remains in the custom of compelling everybody who passes the palace where the Sultan is residing to lower his Umbrella as a mark of respect. And—at all events some years back, before the Crimean war had introduced so many Europeans to Constantinople—any one neglecting to pay the required reverence, stood in considerable danger of a lively reminder from the sentry on duty.

Before concluding this chapter, it may not be out of place to make a few remarks as to the origin of the word Umbrella, as we have done regarding the thing itself. The English name is borrowed from the Italian *Ombrella.* The Latin term *Umbella* is applied by botanists to those blossoms which are clustered at the extremities of several spokes, radiating from the common stem like the metallic props of the Umbrella. The name, as is seen, does not give the slightest idea of the use of the article designated, as is often the case with words we practical folk employ; and we might well take a lesson from our cousins German or French, who have invented distinct names for the weapon used to ward off the rays of the sun, and that employed against rain, namely,—Regenschirm, *parapluie;* Sonnenschirm, *parasol.* These are better than our names, even though both the French words labour under the disadvantage of being hybrids, half Greek and half Latin.

Such, then, is the ancient history of the Umbrella, as far as our research has enabled us to trace it, and, indeed, we are now not a little surprised at the result of those labours which have enabled us to discover so much.

CHAPTER III.

THE UMBRELLA IN ENGLAND.

As a canopy of state, Umbrellas were generally used in the south of Europe; they are found in the ceremonies of the Byzantine Church; they were borne over the Host in procession, and formed part of the Pontifical regalia.

A mediæval gem represents a bishop, attended by a cross-bearer, and a servant who carries behind him an Umbrella.

In the Basilican churches of Rome is suspended a large Umbrella, and the cardinal who took his title from the church has the privilege of having an Umbrella carried over his head on solemn processions. It is not, altogether impossible that the cardinal's hat may be derived from this Umbrella. The origin of this custom of hanging an Umbrella in the Basilican churches is plain enough. The judge sitting in the basilica would have it as part of his insignia of office. On the judgment hall being turned into a church, the Umbrella remained, and in fact occupied the place of the canopy over thrones and the like in our own country. Beatiano, an Italian herald, says that "a vermilion Umbrella in a field argent symbolises dominion."

References crop up now and then throughout the middle age records, to Umbrellas; but the extreme paucity of such allusions goes to show that they were not in common use. In an old romance, "The Blonde of Oxford," a jester makes fun of a nobleman for being out in the rain without his cloak. "Were I a rich man," says he, "I would bear my house about with me." By this very valiant joke he meant, as he afterwards explained, that the nobleman should wear a cloak, not that he ought not to forget his Umbrella So it is clear, we find, that our forefathers depended on their cloaks, not on their Umbrellas, for protection against storms.

Careful research has enabled us to light on a solitary instance of an ancient English Umbrella, for Wright, in his "Domestic Manners of the English," gives a drawing from the Harleian MS., No. 603, which represents an Anglo-Saxon gentleman walking out attended by his servant, the servant carrying an Umbrella with a handle that slopes backwards, so as to bring the Umbrella over the head of the person in front. It probably, therefore, could not be shut up, but otherwise it looks like an ordinary Umbrella, and the ribs are represented distinctly.

Whether this earliest Jonas Hanway (the reputed first importer of the Umbrella, of whom more hereafter) was peculiarly sybaritic in his notions, or whether, like the mammoth of Siberia, he is the one remaining instance of a former "umbrelliferous" race, must, at least for the present, remain undecided. The general use of the Parasol in France and England was adopted, probably from China, about the middle of the seventeenth century. At that period, pictorial representations of it are frequently found, some of which exhibit the peculiar broad and deep canopy belonging to the large Parasol of the Chinese Government officials, borne by native attendants.

John Evelyn, in his Diary for the 22nd June, 1664, mentions a collection of rarities shown him by one Thompson, a Catholic priest, sent by the Jesuits of Japan and China to France. Among the curiosities were "fans like those our ladies use, but much larger, and with long handles, strangely carved and filled with Chinese characters," which is evidently a description of the Parasol.

In the title-page of Evelyn's "Kalendarium Hortense," also published in the same year, we find a black page represented, bearing a closed Umbrella or Sunshade. It is again evident that the Parasol was more an article of curiosity than use at this period, from the fact that it is mentioned as such in the catalogue of the "*Museum Tradescantium*, or Collection of Rarities, preserved at South Lambeth, by London, by John Tradescant."

In Coryat's "Crudities," a very rare and highly interesting work, published in 1611, about a century and a half prior to the general introduction of the Umbrella into England, we find the following curious passage:—

After talking of fans he goes on to say, "And many of them doe carry other fine things of a far greater price, that will cost at the least a duckat, which they commonly call in the Italian tongue umbrellas, that is, things which minister shadow veto them for shelter against the scorching heate of the sunne. These are made of leather, something answerable to the forme of a little cannopy, & hooped in the inside with divers little wooden hoopes that extend the umbrella in a pretty large cornpasse. They are used especially by horsemen, who carry them in their hands when they ride, fastening the end of the handle upon one of their thighs, and they impart so large a shadow unto them, that it keepeth the heate of the sunne from the upper parts of their bodies."

Reference to the same custom, of riders in Italy using umbrellas, is made in Florio's "Worlde of Wordes" (1598), where we find "Ombrella, a fan, a canopie, also a festoon or cloth of State for a prince, also a kind of round fan or shadowing that they use to ride with in sommer in Italy, a little shade."

In Cotgrave's "Dictionary of the French and English Tongues," the French Ombrelle is translated, "An umbrello; a (fashion of) round and broad fanne, wherewith the Indians (and from them our great ones) preserve themselves from the heat of a scorching sunne; and hence any little shadow, fanne, or thing, wherewith women hide their faces fro the sunne."

In Fynes Moryson's "Itinerary" (1617) we find a similar allusion to the habit of carrying Umbrellas in hot countries "to auoide the beames of the sunne." Their employment, says the author, is dangerous, "because they gather the heate into a pyramidall point, and thence cast it down perpendicularly upon the head, except they know how to carry them for auoyding that danger." This is certainly a fact not generally known to those who use Parasols too recklessly.

"Poesis Rediviva," by John Collop, M.D. (1656), mentions Umbrellas. Michael Drayton, writing about 1620, speaks of a pair of doves, which are to watch over the person addressed in his verses:—

"Of doves I have a dainty pair,
Which, when you please to take the air,
About your head shall gently hover,
Your clear brow from the sun to cover;

And with their nimble wings shall fan you,
That neither cold nor heat shall tan you;
And, like umbrellas, with their feathers
Shall shield you in all sorts of weathers."

Beaumont and Fletcher have an allusion to the umbrella (1640);—

"Now are you glad, now is your mind at ease,
Now you have got a shadow, an umbrella,
To keep the 'scorching world's opinion
From your fair credit."
—*Rule a Wife and Have a Wife,* Act iii, sc. I.

Ben Jonson, too, once mentions it (date 1616), speaking of a mishap which befel a lady at the Spanish Court:—

"And there she lay, flat spread as an umbrella."
—*The Devil is an Ass,* Act iv., SC. I.

Of the fact that Umbrellas' were known and used in Italy long prior to their introduction into France, we find a confirmation in old Montaigne, who observes, *lib.* iii. *cap.* ix. :—"Les Ombrelles, de quoy depuis les anciens Remains l'Italie se sert, chargent plus le bras, qu'ils ne deschargent la teste."

Kersey's Dictionary (1708) describes an Umbrella as a "screen commonly used by women to keep off rain."

The absence of almost all allusion to the Umbrella by the wits of the seventeenth century, while the muff, fan, &c., receive so large a share of attention, is a further proof that it was far from being recognised as an article of convenient luxury at that day. The clumsy shape, probably, prevented its being generally used. In one of Dryden's plays we find the line:—

"I can carry your umbrella and fan, your Ladyship."

Gay, addressing a gentleman, in his "Trivia, or the Art of Walking the Streets of London" (1712), says:—

"Be thou for every season justly dress'd,
Nor brave the piercing frost with open breast:
And when the bursting clouds a deluge pour.
Let thy surtout defend the gaping shower."

And again: —

"That garment best the winter's rage defends
Whose shapeless form in ample plaits depends;
By various names in various countries known,
Yet held in all the true surtout alone.
Be thine of kersey tine, though small the cost,
Then brave, unwet, the rain, unchilled, the frost."

These passages lead us to the belief that the Umbrella was not used by gentlemen for a long time after its merits had been recognised by the fair sex.

The following lines from the same author have often been quoted: —

"Good housewives all the winter's rage despise
Defended by the riding-hood's disguise:
Or underneath the umbrella's oily shed
Safe through the wet on clinking pattens tread.
Let Persian dames th' umbrellas rich display,
To guard their beauties from the sunny ray,
Or sweating slaves support the shady load,
When Eastern monarchs show their state abroad,
Britain in winter only knows its aid
To guard from chilly showers the walking maid."
—*Trivia*, B. 1.

Dean Swift, also, in the *Tatler*, No. 228, in describing a City shower, thus alludes to the common use of the Umbrella by women: —

"Now in contiguous drops the floods come down,
Threatening with deluge the devoted town:

To shops in crowds the draggled females fly,
Pretend to cheapen goods, but nothing buy:
The Templar spruce, while every spout's abroach,
Stays till 'tis fair, yet seems to call a coach:
The tucked-up sempstress walks with hasty strides,
While streams run down her oiled umbrella's sides."

About this time the custom obtained of keeping an Umbrella in the halls of great houses, to be used in passing from the door to the carriage. At coffee-houses, too, the same was done.

That the use of the Umbrella was considered far too effeminate for man, is seen from the following advertisement from the *Female Tatler* for December 12th, 1709:—"The young gentleman borrowing the Umbrella belonging to Wills' Coffee-house, in Cornhill, of the mistress, is hereby advertised, that to be dry from head to foot on the like occasion, he shall be welcome to the maid's pattens."

Defoe's description of Robinson Crusoe's Umbrella is, of course, familiar to all our readers. He makes his hero say that he had seen Umbrellas used in Brazil, where they were found very useful in the great heats that were there, and that he constructed his own instrument in imitation of them, "I covered it with skins," he adds, "the hair outwards, so that it cast off the rain like a pent-house, and kept off the sun so effectually, that I could walk out in the hottest of the weather with greater advantage than I could before in the coolest." We may also add, that from this description the original heavy Umbrellas obtained the name of "Robinson," which they retained for many years, both here and in France.

In the "Memoir of Ambrose Barnes," published for the Surtees Society, under date 1718, appears an entry, "Umbrella for the Church's use, 25s." A similar entry is also found in the churchwarden's accounts for the parochial chapelry of Burnley, Surrey, for A.D. 1760, "Paid for Umbrella 2_l_. 10_s_. 6_d_." Both these Umbrellas were in all likelihood intended for the use of clergymen at funerals in the churchyard, as was that alluded to in Hone's *Year-Book* (1826) which was kept for the same purpose in a country church. This last had "an awning of green oiled canvas, such as common Umbrellas were made of, forty years ago."

Bailey's *Encyclopædia* (1736) has "Umbrello, a sort of wooden frame, covered with cloth, put over a window to keep out the sun; also a screen carried over the head to defend from sun or rain." Also "Parasol, a little umbrella to keep off sun."

There is at Woburn Abbey a picture, painted about 1730, of the Duchess of Bedford, with a black servant behind her, who holds an Umbrella over her, and a sketch of the same period attached to a song called "The Generous Repulse," shows a lady seated on a flowery bank holding a Parasol with a long handle over her head, while she gently checks the ardour of her swain, and consoles him by the following touching strain:—

"Thy vain pursuit, fond youth, give o'er,
What more, alas! can Flavia do?
Thy worth I own, thy fate deplore,
All are not happy that are true."

* * * * *

"But if revenge can ease thy pain,
I'll soothe the ills I cannot cure,
Tell thee I drag a hopeless chain,
And all that I inflict endure!"

Rather cold consolation, but an unexceptionable and moral sentiment.

The idea, therefore, that the Duchess of Rutland devised Parasols in 1826 for the first time is obviously incorrect, whatever her grace may have done towards rendering them fashionable. Captain Cook, in one of his voyages, saw some of the natives of the South Pacific Islands, with Umbrellas made of palm-leaves.

We have thus seen that the use both of the Umbrella and Parasol was not unknown in England during the earlier half of the eighteenth century. That it was not very common, is evident from the fact that General (then Lieut.-Colonel) Wolfe, writing from Paris in 1752, speaks of the people there using Umbrellas for the sun and rain, and wonders that a similar practice does not obtain in England.

Just about the same time they do seem to have come into general use, and that pretty rapidly, as people found their value, and got over the shyness natural to a first introduction. Jonas Hanway, the founder of the Magdalen Hospital, has the credit of being the first man who had the courage to carry one habitually in London, since it is recorded in the life of that venerable philanthropist, the friend of chimney-sweeps and sworn foe to tea, that he was the first man who ventured to dare public reproach and ridicule by carrying an Umbrella. He probably felt the benefit of one during his travels in Persia, where they were in constant use as a protection against the sun, and it is also said that he was in ill health when he first made use of it. It was more than likely, however, that Jonas Hanway's neatness in dress and delicate complexion led him, on his return from abroad, to appreciate a luxury hitherto only confined to the ladies. Mr. Pugh, who wrote his life, gives the following description of his personal appearance, which may be regarded as a gem in its way:—

"In his dress, as far as was consistent with his ideas of health and ease, he accommodated himself to the prevailing fashion. As it was frequently necessary for him to appear in polite circles on unexpected occasions, he usually wore dress clothes with a large French bag. His hat, ornamented with a gold button, was of a size and fashion to be worn as well under the arm as on the head. When it rained, a small *parapluie* defended his face and wig."

As Hanway died in 1786, and he is said to have carried an Umbrella for thirty years, the date of its first use by him may be set down at about 1750. For some time Umbrellas were objects of derision, especially from the hackney coachmen, who saw in their use an invasion on the vested rights of the fraternity; just as hackney coaches had once been looked upon by the watermen, who thought people should travel by river, not by road. John Macdonald, perhaps the only footman (always excepting the great Mr. James Yellowplush) who ever wrote a memoir of himself, relates that in 1770, he used to be greeted with the shout, "Frenchman, Frenchman! why don't you call a coach?" whenever he went out with his "fine silk umbrella, newly brought from Spain." Records of the Umbrella's first appearance in other English works have also been preserved. In Glasgow (according to the narrative in Cleland's "Statistical Account of Glasgow ") "the late Mr. John Jamieson, surgeon, returning from Paris, brought an Umbrella with him, which was the first seen in this city. The doctor, who was a man of great humour, took pleasure in relating to me how he was stared at with his Umbrella." In Edinburgh Dr. Spens is said to have been the first to carry one. In Bristol a red Leghorn Umbrella appeared about 1780, according to a writer in *Notes and Queries,* and created there no small sensation. The trade between Bristol and Leghorn may account for this. Some five-and-thirty years ago it is said that an old lady was living in Taunton who recollected when there were only two Umbrellas in the town, one of which belonged to the clergyman. When he went to church, he used to hang the Umbrella up in the porch, to the edification and delight of his parishioners.

Horace Walpole tells how Dr. Shebbeare (who was prosecuted for seditious writings in 1758) "stood in the pillory, having a footman holding an umbrella to keep off the rain." For permitting this indulgence to a malefactor, Beardman, the under-sheriff, was punished.

It is difficult to conceive how the Umbrella could come into general use, owing to the state in which the streets of London were up to a comparatively recent period. The same amusing author to whom we owe the description of Jonas Hanway, gives the following account of them at the time his work was published:—

"It is not easy to convey to a person who has not seen the streets of London before they were uniformly paved, a tolerable idea of their inconvenience and uncleanliness; the signs extending on both sides of the way into the streets, at unequal distances from the houses, that they might not intercept each other, greatly obstructed the view; and, what is of more consequence in a crowded city, prevented the free circulation of the air. The footpaths were universally incommoded—even when they were so narrow as only to admit one person passing at a time—by a row of posts set on edge next the carriage-way. He whose urgent business would not permit of his keeping pace with the gentleman of leisure before him, turned out between the two posts before the door of some large house into the carriage-way. When he perceived danger moving toward him, he wished to return within the protection of the row of posts; but there was commonly a rail continued from the top of one post to that of another, sometimes for several houses together, in which case he was obliged to run back to the first inlet, or climb over, or creep under the railing, in attempting which, he might be fortunate if he escaped with no other injury than what proceeded from dirt; if, intimidated by the danger he escaped, he afterwards kept within the boundary of the posts and railing, he was obliged to put aside the travellers before him, whose haste was less urgent than his, and, these resisting, made his journey truly a warfare.

"The French are reproached, even to a proverb, for the neglect of the convenience of foot-passengers in their metropolis, by not providing a separate path for them; but, great as is the exposure to dirt in Paris, for want of a footpath, which their many *porte-cochères* seem likely for ever to prevent, in the more important article of danger, the City of London was, at this period, at least on a par. How comfortless must be the sensations of an unfortunate female, stopped in the street on a windy day under a large old sign loaded with lead and iron in full swing over, her head? and perhaps a torrent of rain and dirty water falling near from a projecting spout, ornamented with the mouth and teeth of a dragon. These dangers and distresses are now at an end; and we may think of them as a sailor does of a storm, which has subsided, but the advantages derived from the present uniformity and cleanliness can be known only in their full extent by comparing them with the former inconveniences."

When to this description is added the fact that the hoop petticoat and another article of dress monopolised the whalebone, it will be seen how much had to be got over before an Umbrella could be carried out by the citizens of London, as a walking-staff, with satisfactory assurance of protection in case of a shower. The earliest English Umbrellas, we must also remember, were made of oiled silk, very clumsy and difficult to open when wet; the stick and furniture were heavy and inconvenient, and the article very expensive.

At the end of the century allusions to the Umbrella are not infrequent. Cowper, in his "Task" (1780), twice mentions it, but seems to mean a Parasol:—

"We bear our shades about us; self-deprived
Of other screen, the thin umbrella spread,

And range an Indian waste without a tree."
—B. i.

And again:—

"Expect her soon, with footboy at her heels,
No longer blushing for her awkward load,
Her train and her umbrella all her care."
—B. iv,

The Rev. G. C. Renouard, writing in 1850 to Notes and Queries, says:—

"In the hall of my father's house, at Stamford, in Lincolnshire, there was, when I was a child, the wreck of a large green silk umbrella, apparently of Chinese manufacture, brought by my father from Scotland, somewhere between 1770 and 1780, and, as I have often heard, the first umbrella seen at Stamford. I well remember, also, an amusing description given by the late Mr. Warry, so many years consul at Smyrna, of the astonishment and envy of his mother's neighbours, at Sawbridgeworth, in Hants, where his father had a country house, when he ran home and came back with an umbrella, which he had just brought from Leghorn, to shelter them from a pelting shower which detained them in the church porch, after the service, on one summer Sunday. From Mr. Warry's age at the time he mentioned this, and other circumstances in his history, I conjecture that it occurred not later than 1775 or 1776. As Sawbridgeworth is so near London, it is evident that even then umbrellas were at that time almost unknown."

Since this date, however, the Umbrella has come into general use, and in consequence numerous improvements have been effected in it. The transition to the present portable form is due, partly to the substitution of silk and gingham for the heavy and troublesome oiled silk, which admitted of the ribs and frames being made much lighter, and also to the many ingenious mechanical improvements in the framework, chiefly by French and English manufacturers, many of which were patented, and to which we purpose presently to allude.

CHAPTER IV.

THE STORY OF THE PARACHUTE.

In giving an account of the Umbrella, it would not be right to omit mentioning another, and far from legitimate use in which it has been employed by notoriety-hunting *artistes*—we allude to the Parachute; and a short narration of its origin and progress may not be uninteresting to our readers.

The Parachute commonly in use is nothing more or less than a huge Umbrella, presenting a surface of sufficient dimension to experience from the air a resistance equal to the weight of descent, in moving through the fluid at a velocity not exceeding that of the shock which a person can sustain without danger or injury. It is made of silk or cotton. To the outer edge cords are fastened, of about the same length as the diameter of the machine (24 to 28 feet). A centre cord is attached to the apex and meets the cords from the margin, acting, in fact, as the stick of the Umbrella. The machine is thus kept expanded during descent. The car is fastened to the centre cord, and the whole attached to the balloon in such a manner that it may be readily and quickly detached, either by cutting a string, or pulling a trigger. Consequently, in the East, where the Umbrella has been from the earliest ages in familiar use, it appears to have been occasionally employed by vaulters, to enable them to jump safely from great heights. Father Loubère, in his curious account of Siam, relates, that a person famous in that country for his dexterity, used to divert the King and Court by the extraordinary leaps he took, having two Umbrellas with long slender handles, fastened to his girdle. In 1783 M. le Normand demonstrated the utility of the Parachute; by lifting himself down from the windows of a high house at Lyons. His idea was that it might be made a sort of fire-escape.

Blanchard was the first person who constructed a Parachute to act as a safety-guard to the aeronaut in case of any accident. During an excursion he made from Lille, in 1785, when he traversed, without stopping, a distance of 300 miles, he let down a Parachute with a basket fastened to it containing a dog. This he suffered to fall from a great height, and it reached the ground in safety.

The first Parachute descent from a balloon, however, was made by Jacques Garnerin, on the 22nd of October, 1797, in the Park of Monceau. De la Lande, the celebrated astronomer, has furnished a detailed and highly interesting account of this foolish experiment.

Garnerin resided in London during the short peace of 1802, and made two ascents with his balloon, in the second of which he let himself fall, at an amazing height, with a Parachute of 23 feet diameter. He started from an enclosure near North Audley Street, and descended after having been seven or eight minutes in the air. After cutting himself away, he floated over Marylebone and Somers Town, and fell in a field near St. Pancras Old Church. The oscillation was so great, that he was thrown out of the Parachute, and narrowly escaped death. He seemed a good deal frightened, and said that the peril was too great for endurance. One of the stays of the machine having given way, his danger was increased. The next person who tried this dangerous experiment was his niece, Eliza Garnerin, who descended several times in safety. Her Parachute had a large orifice in the top, in order to check the oscillation, and this appears to have been tolerably successful.

The next experimentalist was a person of the name of Cocking, who ended his days in a manner unworthy his talents, through a series of lamentable mistakes. His Parachute was constructed on the opposite principle, of a wedge-like form, and was intended to cleave through the air, instead of offering a resistance to it. It has not yet been proved that the principle was wrong, but the defect lay in the weakness of the materials employed in the formation of the Parachute.

On the 29th July, 1837, Mr. Cocking ascended in his new Parachute, attached to the Great Nassau Balloon. Mr. Cocking liberated himself from the balloon, the Parachute collapsed and fell, at a frightful rate, into a field near Lea, where poor Cocking was found with an awful wound on his right temple. He never spoke, but died almost immediately afterwards. It is much to be regretted that the descent was ever allowed to take place. The aeronauts themselves were for some time in a state of imminent peril. Immediately the Parachute was cut away, the balloon ascended with frightful velocity, owing to the ascending power it necessarily gained by being freed from a weight of nearly 500 pounds; and had it not been that its occupants applied their mouths to the air-bags previously provided, they must have been suffocated by the escaping gas. When the re-action took place, the balloon had lost its buoyancy, and fell, rather than descended, to the ground.

Mr. Hampton was the next person who attempted the experiment, and made three descents in a Parachute in succession without injury. Undeterred by the awful fate of his predecessor, this gentleman determined on making a Parachute descent which should prove the correctness of the theory, and the Montpellier Gardens at Cheltenham were selected as the scene of the exploit. Owing to the censure which was attached to the proprietors of the Vauxhall Gardens, for permitting docking's ascent, the owners of the Gardens at Cheltenham would not suffer the experiment to be made, and Mr. Hampton was obliged to have recourse to stratagem. As he was permitted to display his Parachute in the manner he intended to use it, the idea suddenly flashed across his mind that, he could carry out his long-nursed wishes. He suddenly cut the rope which kept him down, and went off, to the astonishment of the spectators. the last cheering sound that reached him being—"He will be killed to a dead certainty!"

After attaining an altitude of nearly two miles, Mr. Hampton proceeded to cut the rope that held him attached to the balloon. He paused for a second or two, as he remembered that it would soon be life or death with him, but at length drew his knife across the rope. The first feelings he experienced were both unpleasant and alarming; his eyes and the top of his head appeared to be forced upwards, but this passed off in a few seconds, and his feelings subsequently became pleasant, rather than disagreeable.

So steady and slow was the descent that the Parachute appeared to be stationary. Mr. Hampton remembered that a bag of ballast was fastened beneath the car, he stooped over and upset the sand, he also noted by his watch the time he occupied in descending. The earth seemed coming up to him rapidly; the Parachute indicated its approach to *terra, firma* by a slight oscillation, and he presently struck the ground in the centre of a field, where he was first welcomed by a sheep, which stared at this visitor from the clouds in utter amazement. Mr. Hampton repeated the experiment twice in London, though on both occasions with considerable danger to himself, the first time falling on a tree in Kensington Gardens, the second on a house, which threw him out of the basket.

After this experiment there was a lull in the Parachute folly until some twenty years ago, when Madame Poitevin startled the Metropolis from its propriety by her perilous escapes both in life and limb. Although considerable ingenuity was displayed in the plan of expanding the Parachute by the sudden discharge of gas from the balloon; still the very fact of a woman being exposed to such danger by her husband, will, we trust, hereafter prevent Englishmen from countenancing such an exhibition by their presence.

CHAPTER V.

UMBRELLA STORIES.

Who could for a moment suppose that so important an article as the Umbrella would be without its lighter as well as its more serious history? Umbrellas are still, we regret to say, regarded rather in a comic than a serious light; so, if any of the following anecdotes seem to treat of Umbrellas in too mocking or frivolous a vein, it is the fault of the bad taste of the British public, not ours, who have merely compiled. However, we may commence with a very neat little French riddle.

"Quel est l'objet que l'on recherche le plus quand on s'en dégoûte?"

A mysterious inquiry, and all sorts of horrible but needful abominations occur to the mind in answer. But the answer is not so bad after all. Change the spelling without altering the pronunciation, and you get *quand on sent des gouties*, and, lo! you have it at once—le Parapluie—the faithful friend whose presence we most desire when we wish least for the necessity of it; the burden of our fine days, the shelter of our wet ones.

Or again, would you like a verse or two on the same subject?

"Pour étrenne, on veut à l'envie
Du frais et du neuf et du beau,
Je dis que c'est un parapluie,
Que l'on doit donner en *cas d'eau.*"

The author of these two *jeux de mots* unhappily we do not know, or we would thank him for them. The English poet of the Umbrella has yet to be born.

The next story relates to the early history of the Umbrella in Scotland, and may probably be referred to the time when good Dr. Jamieson was walking about Glasgow with his new-fangled sheltering apparatus, which he had brought with him on his return from Paris. As it was the first ever seen in that city, it attracted universal attention, and a vast amount of impudence from the "horrid boys." The following anecdote, then, which we borrow from a Scotch paper, most probably refers to the same period, or thereabouts :—

"When Umbrellas were first marched into Blairgowrie, they were sported only by the minister and the laird, and were looked upon by the common class of people as a perfect phenomenon. One day Daniel M— went to Colonel McPherson, at Blairgowrie House; when about to return, a shower came on, and the colonel politely offered him the loan of an Umbrella, which he gladly accepted, and Daniel, with his head two or three inches higher than usual, marched off. Not long after he had left, however, the colonel again saw Daniel posting towards him with all possible haste, still o'ertopped by his cotton canopy (silk Umbrellas were out of the question in those days), which he held out, saluting him with—' Hae, hae, Kornil, this'll never do! there's nae a door in all my house that'll tak it in; my very barn-door winna' tak it in.'"

In the veracious "History of Sandford and Merton," if our memory serves us aright, there is an instance quoted of remarkable presence of mind relating to an Umbrella and its owner. The members of a comfortable pic-nic party were cosily assembled in some part of India, when an unbidden and most unwelcome guest made his appearance, in the shape of a huge Bengal tiger. Most persons would, naturally, have sought safety in flight, and not stayed to hob-and-nob with this denizen of the jungle; not so, however, thought a lady of the party, who, inspired by her innate courage, or the fear of losing her dinner —perhaps by both combined seized her Umbrella, and opened it suddenly in the face of the tiger as he stood wistfully gazing upon brown curry and foaming Allsop. The astonished brute turned tail and fled, and the lady saved her dinner. Not many years ago the Umbrella was employed in an equally curious manner, though not so successfully as in the former instance. In the campaign of 1793, General Bournonville, who was sent with four commissioners by the National Convention to the camp of the Prince of Saxe-Coburg, was detained as a prisoner with his companions, and confined in the fortress of Olmütz. In this situation he made a desperate attempt to regain his liberty. Having procured an Umbrella, he leaped with it from a window forty feet above the ground, but being a very heavy man, it did not prove sufficient to let him down in safety. He struck against an opposite wall, fell into a ditch and broke his leg, and, worse than all, was carried back to his prison.

One of the most remarkable instances on record, in which the Umbrella was the agency of a man's life being saved, occurred, according to his own statement, to our old friend Colonel Longbow. Of course our kind readers know him as well as we do, for not to do so "would be to argue yourselves unknown." At any Continental watering place, Longbow, or one of his family—for it is a large one—can be met with. He is, indeed, a wonderful man—on intimate terms with all the crowned heads of Europe, and proves his intimacy by always speaking of them by their Christian names.

He is at once the "guide, philosopher, and friend" of every stranger who happens to form his acquaintance—a very easy task, be it remarked—and, though so great a man, is not above dining at your expense, and charming you by the terms of easy familiarity with which he imbibes your champagne or your porter, for all is alike to him, so long as he has not to pay for it: he can take any given quantity.

Well, the other day we happened to meet the Colonel, and he speedily contrived to discover that we were on the point of going to dine, and so invited him to share our humble meal, as a graceful way of making a virtue of necessity, for had we not done so, he would have had no hesitation in inviting himself. During dinner, conversation, of course, turned upon one all-engrossing subject, the war, and the Colonel proceeded to give us his experiences of former wars, including his adventures in the Crimea, and the miraculous escape he owed to an Umbrella.

It appeared that he had gone out with his friend, Lord Levant, on a yachting excursion in the Mediterranean, and they eventually found their way into the Black Sea. Stress of weather compelled them to put into the little port of Yalta, on the north coast, where they went on shore. The Colonel, on the Lucretian principle of "Suave mari magno," &c., proceeded the next morning to the verge of the precipice to observe the magnificent prospect of a sea running mountains high. As it was raining at the time, he put up a huge gingham Umbrella he happened to find in the hotel. Suddenly, however, a furious blast of wind drove across the cliff, and lifted the Colonel bodily in the air. Away he flew far out to sea, the Umbrella acting as a Parachute to let him fall easy.

Now to most men this would only have been a choice of evils, a progress from Scylla to Charybdis: not so to our Colonel. On coming up to the surface after his first dip, he found that swimming would not save him; so he quietly emptied out the water contained in the Umbrella, seated himself upon it, and sailed triumphantly into the harbour, like Arion on his dolphin.

Our face, on hearing this anecdote, must have betrayed the scepticism we felt, for the Colonel proceeded to a corner of the room, and produced the identical Umbrella. Of course, such a proof was irresistible, and we were compelled to do penance for our unbelief by lending the gallant Colonel a sovereign, for "the Bank was closed." We thought the anecdote cheap at the price.

There is a story told of one of our City bankers, that he owed an excellent wife to the interposition of an Umbrella. It appears that on returning home one day in a heavy shower of rain, he found a young lady standing in his doorway. Politeness induced him to invite her to take shelter under his roof, and eventually to offer her the loan of an Umbrella. Of course, the gallant banker called for it the next day, and the acquaintance thus accidentally made, soon ripened into mutual affection. This species of Umbrella courtship has been immortalised in more than one song, none of which, however, are quite worth quoting.

A worthy little Frenchman of our acquaintance was ordered by his medical man to take a course of shower-baths. Such things being unknown to him in his fatherland, he of course found the first essay remarkably unpleasant, but with native ingenuity he soon discovered a remedy. On our asking him how he liked the hydropathic system, he replied, "Oh, mais c'est charmant, mon ami; I always take my parapluie wid me into de bath."

Douglas Jerrold, in his well-known "Punch's Letters to his Son," gives an anecdote of which we can only say, si non *è vero, è ben trovato*. It at all events illustrates the frightful morality that exists with regard to borrowing Umbrellas.

"Hopkins once lent Simpson, his next-door neighbour, an Umbrella. You will judge of the intellect of Hopkins, not so much from the act of lending an Umbrella, but from his insane endeavour to get it back again.

"It poured in torrents, Hopkins had an urgent call. Hopkins knocked at Simpson's door. 'I want my Umbrella.' Now Simpson had also a call in a directly opposite way to Hopkins; and with the borrowed Umbrella in his hand, was advancing to the threshold. 'I tell you,' roared Hopkins, 'I want my Umbrella.' 'Can't have it,' said Simpson. 'Why, I want to go to the East-end; it rains in torrents; what'—screamed Hopkins—'what am I to do for an Umbrella?'

"'Do!' answered Simpson, darting from the door, 'do as I did—
BORROW
ONE.'"

The Umbrella has been most successfully introduced on the stage. What, for instance, would Paul Pry have been without that valuable implement for which to inquire with his stereotyped "Hope I don't intrude?" Or his French successor, the nobleman in "The Grand Duchess," who inquires, in plaintive accents, for "Le parapluie de ma mere," just after Schneider has been declaiming about her father's sabre? Merely to bring a big Umbrella on the stage is an acknowledged way of raising a laugh. Mrs. Gamp again, with her receptacle for unconsidered trifles, cannot be realised apart from her Umbrella. And then, those hired waiters who come into our houses with an Umbrella of graceful proportions, and emerge towards the small hours with a most plethoric parapluie, which looks as if it had been regaling on the good things as well as its master! It used to appear to us a comical sight, years back, in the old city of Paris, to see the National Guard going to exercise with a musket in one hand and an Umbrella in the other, and we dare say it was a very sensible plan after all, and might have been imitated with success before Sebastopol. A stout steel Umbrella would offer no contemptible shelter to a rifleman. This circumstance, too, may throw a light on a hitherto obscure passage in "Macbeth," where Birnam Wood moves to Dunsinane—for it is just possible that the soldiers cut down the branches to serve them as a protection from the rain. We throw out this as a hint to any enterprising manager.

In Germany, on the other hand, a soldier is—or used to be—strictly forbidden from carrying an open Umbrella, unless he is accompanied by a civilian or a lady. A worthy corporal, on one occasion, was sent to fetch an Umbrella his Major's lady had left at a friend's house, and at the same time took her lapdog for an airing. On the road home a violent shower came on, and, to avoid committing a breach of the regulations, under his arm he tucked the dog, which was contained, according to his ideas, in both the above categories, put up the Umbrella, and marched very comfortably to barracks.

With one more characteristic anecdote we will close our budget. One evening, while Rowland Hill was preaching, a shower came on, and his chapel was speedily filled with devotees. With that peculiar sarcastic intonation which none could assume so successfully as himself, he quietly remarked, "My brethren, I have often heard that religion can be made a *cloak*, but this is the first occasion on which I ever knew it could be converted into an *Umbrella*."

CHAPTER VI.

THE REGENERATION OF THE UMBRELLA.

Our task is now nearly completed: we have described the history of the Parasol, and its near relation the Umbrella, as far as our space permits us to treat of this interesting subject.

All that remains for us to do is to give an account of the principal improvements effected in the Umbrella during later years.

It is certain that France was some way ahead of us with regard to the use of Umbrellas, for they were comparatively common there before they were at all known *l'autre côté 'de la Manche*. This was but natural, considering that they were, as we have seen, used in Italy, and consequently the folk of southern France would not be likely to be far behind their neighbours in availing themselves of the protection from the sun, whether or no they had sufficient genius to shelter themselves from the rain by the aid of an Umbrella.

In France Parasols and Umbrellas used to be amongst the articles made by the corporate body of Boursiers. M. Natalis Rondot quotes from the *Journal du Citoyen*, of 1754, the price of Parasols. It ranged from 7s. 3_d_. to 17s. 6_d_., according to the construction, and to whether they were made to fold up or not. In Diderot and D'Alembert's Encyclopédic, is figured an Umbrella, which is described as follows, in the excellent introduction to the "Abridgements of Specifications relating to Umbrellas," lately published by the Commissioners of Patents:—

"The ribs bear about the same proportion (as in modern umbrellas) as regards length, to the stick, but the stretchers are much shorter, being less than a quarter of the length of the ribs. They are double, each rib having a pair joined, one on each side of the rib, at the same point. The ribs are joined at the top by being strung on a ring, as in old English umbrellas, but the runner is made of precisely similar construction to the modern runner, and seems almost identical with that described in Caney's Specification (patent No. 5761, A.D. 1829). Ribs and sticks are jointed, the latter in two places. There is no catch to hold the umbrella closed, but this upper catch is the ordinary bent wire one. The upper joint of the stick is made with a screw, the lower of a hinge with a slide, as in a modern parasol. The slide has a catch, resembling the ordinary runner catch. At the top is a ring for carrying or suspending the umbrella."

Such was the old French Umbrella, and that used in England was of much the same sort. The old French folding Parasol is thus described in the "Report of the Jurors for the Exhibition of 1851:"—

"The folding parasol was constructed with jointed ribs so as to fold back, and was likewise self-opening. The rod was a metallic tube, and contained a spiral spring which acted upon and pressed upwards an inner rod. To this inner rod were jointed the stretchers, which in this construction were placed above the ribs instead of below, as in the ordinary form, beside which they were much shorter, so as to admit of their being concealed by the covering. By the elasticity of the spiral spring contained in the hollow stem, the inner rod was pressed outwards and lifted the stretchers, and by their means raised the ribs also, so that in its ordinary or natural state the umbrella was always open, and would continue so unless constrained to remain closed by a catch. On releasing the catch it consequently sprang open. In order that it might be easily closed, four cords were attached to four of the ribs and passed to the handle; and a loop embracing these cords passed down by the side of the handle, and enabled the possessor to close his umbrella without difficulty. From the authority already quoted, we learn that whalebone was employed for the ribs, and that their number varied with their length; for example, when 24 inches long the number employed was 8; when 25 inches, 9; and when 26, 28 and 30 inches, 10 were used. Calico was employed to cover umbrellas, and silk to cover parasols. The use of parasols was common in Lyons at that period (1786); they were carried by men as well as women; they were rose-coloured, white, and of other colours, and were so light as to be carried without inconvenience."

The "Encyclopedic Méthodique" gives some interesting particulars as to the manufacture of Parasols and Umbrellas at the end of the eighteenth century. From it, it appears that the ribs were occasionally made of metal. "On étend cette couverture portative par le moyen de quelques brins de baleine, ou de fils de cuivre ou de fer qui la soutiennent." This is interesting, as showing that metal ribs are not a very modern invention.

The following statement of the comparative weights and sizes of Umbrellas was prepared by M. Farge for the French Exposition of 1849: —

Umbrellas Length of ribs. Weight, of inches. Lb. oz.

1645 31 1/2 3 8 1/2 1740 29 1 13 1780 28 3/4 1 8 1/2 1840 27 1/2 0 13 1/4 1849 27 0 8 3/4

From 1808 to 1848, eighty patents were taken out in France for inventions, three of importation, and forty-one for improvements in Umbrellas.

In England, after their first introduction, the manufacture of Um brellas increased rapidly. The first patent is dated 1780, and was taken up by Mark Bull for "A machine for supporting an Umbrella, which may be fixt to any saddle or wheel'd carriage, being far more compleat than any hitherto invented." The invention is described in the following words : —

"There is a ball and socket of steel or iron, or any other metal or composition. The ball moves in any direction, and is fixed by one, two, three, or more points, which are forced against it either by a screw or spring, The ball is made with small cavities to receive the points which press against it. In order to secure it the more effectually in the ball, there is a hole which receives the one end of the staff of the umbrella, which is secured in it either by a spring or screw, or a sliding or a spring bolt. The umbrella may be taken away from the staff; and either put under the seat of the saddle, or fix'd before the rider. The staff may be made whole or in two pieces, the one to slide within the other, in order to raise or lower the umbrella, and be fix'd either by a spring or screw. They are fix'd in the head of the saddle and cover'd by a top, without making the saddle appear in the least different to what they are now made."

The next is of the date of 1786, and was taken out by John Beale for "An umbrella with joints, flat springs, and stops, worm springs and bolts, slip bolts, screws, slip rivet, and cross stop and square slips, and the manner in which the same are performed is particularly described in the several plans, figures, or drawings annexed." The drawings referred to are not easily intelligible, from the briefness of the explanation attached, but show an Umbrella with a jointed handle, opening by a spring.

In the next year (1787) we find an advertisement put out by Thomas Folgham, of Cheapside, stating that he has "a great assortment of his much-approved pocket and portable umbrellas, which for lightness, elegance, and strength, far exceed anything of the kind ever imported or manufactured in this kingdom. All kinds of common umbrellas prepared in a particular way, that will never stick together."

A description of the Umbrellas which, in all probability, Mr. Thomas
Folgham made, we extract from the source mentioned above.

"The early Umbrellas were made of oiled silk, or glazed cotton cloth, and were very cumbrous and inconvenient. To judge from a picture of Hanway, and from the other old pictures mentioned above, they were small, with a very long handle. They were not used for walking, and consequently instead of the ferrule had a ring at the top, by which they were hung up. The stretchers were of cane, and the ribs of cane or whalebone. Instead of the present top-notch and runner, both ribs and stretchers were simply strung on a ring of wire, and the inequality of the friction and the weakness of such an arrangement cause the Umbrella to be always getting out of order. The ribs and stretchers were jointed together very roughly, by a pin passing through the rib, on which the forked end of the stretcher hinged. The first improvement in this respect was by Caney (patent No. 5761, A.D. 1829), who invented a top-notch and runner in which each rib or stretcher has a separate hinge. The top-notch was made of a notched wheel or disc, into each slot of which an axis fixed on the top of the stretchers worked. The runner was made on a similar principle. At the point of the rib where the stretcher joined it, Caney fixed a middle bit, consisting of a small fork, in which the end of the stretcher was hinged. This construction was much stronger, and the forked ends of the stretchers were thus prevented from wearing out the cover, as before. With modifications, more or less important, this construction is the same as that now in general use."

The principal object of all those who have devoted their attention to the task has been to reduce the weight of the Umbrella without, at the same time, diminishing its strength. In its primitive form the ribs were formed of whalebone, which possessed very grave inconveniences; in the first place, it was cumbersome to a degree, lost its elasticity after any continuous exposure to rain, and if dried without very great care, was extremely liable to crack. In the next place, the price was very high, and, consequently, the masses remained unrepresented in the Umbrella market. The most important improvement dates from the introduction of steel instead of whalebone, which took place about thirty years ago, for although a few Umbrellas were occasionally made and used of this material prior to that time, it had not come into general use. Amongst other improvements have been the following: –

The tips are now made in one piece with the rib, instead of being made of bone, japanned metal or other material, and then fastened on. The long six-inch runners have given way to the short one two inches long, and the ferrules are also much shorter than formerly. To keep the Umbrella closed the old-fashioned plan was a ring fastened by a string. A tape and cotton superseded this, and in its turn gave way to the elastic now in use. Sliding caps to fit over the ends of the ribs and hold the Umbrella closed, have been invented, but until quite recently do not seem to have come much into use.

Simple as the construction of an Umbrella may appear, there have been altogether upwards of three hundred patents taken out for various improvements in their manufacture, in addition to numerous alterations which have been registered according to the Act, Vic. 6 & 7, Cap. 65. With very few exceptions the inventors have not been repaid the cost of their patents. This has arisen, partly from the delicacy of their mechanical construction, unfitted for the rough usage to which Umbrellas are exposed; but chiefly in consequence of the increased cost of manufacture not being compensated by the improvements effected.

The introduction of steel vice whalebone, was opposed by the trade and the public in general, like many other great improvements; and it required several years in order to convince purchasers that steel would not only last much longer than whalebone, but would not be so liable to break, provided it was properly made and tempered. The misfortune was that, at the outset, a great number of inferior articles were introduced, and consequently the public naturally lost confidence, and it demanded great exertions on the part of the more respectable members of the trade, ere the merits of the new invention were recognised. At present, it is generally allowed that a good steel-rib Umbrella can be as easily procured as a carefully tempered razor or sword.

A Swiss watch-spring maker, named Sanguinede, had discovered a secret of tempering steel which gave it great strength, and he had made some, very light umbrellas, but they were immensely dear. On his death the secret died with him, and Mr. Fox set to work to discover a method which should combine strength and lightness.

Mr. Fox's Paragon frame, simple in its construction, half the weight of whalebone, but equally strong, is admitted to be the greatest improvement yet introduced in the manufacture of an Umbrella. The ribs are made in the form of a trough with flat sides, by which shape the greatest amount of strength is obtained. The same principle, as is well known, has been successfully applied in the construction of the Great Tubular Bridge over the Menai Straits, from which Mr. Fox took the idea.

The weight of the Umbrella having been thus reduced, the next question was, whether some amendment could not be made in the covering material. For a long time, Umbrellas were only covered with two materials—silk and cotton, and the want of some substance, which would resist the greater friction and consequent wear than an Umbrella invariably undergoes, formed a subject of anxious attention to the writer of this little book. Several materials were tried without success, until a fabric called Alpaca, made of the wool of the Chilian and Peruvian sheep, presented itself, and for this a patent was immediately taken out. Of its merits it becomes us not to speak, but we may be permitted to quote the following remarks from the Grand Jury Report of the Great Exhibition of 1851:—

"SANGSTER, WILLIAM AND JOHN. Prize Medal for Silk Parasols and Umbrellas of excellent quality, 'and for their application of Alpaca cloth to the coverings of Parasols and Umbrellas."

To the above flattering testimonial the following remarks were appended:—

"Alpaca cloth is made of undyed wool of the Peruvian and Chili sheep, and it is therefore is not liable to fade, nor is it acted upon by salt water; hence Alpaca Parasols and Umbrellas are much used at watering-places.

"The demand for the Paragon Umbrella is so great, that the patentee is able to supply them at a price not much exceeding the ordinary sorts. The frames are guaranteed for two years, but in consequence of the superior quality of the article, the number found to require repair is much less than the average of other kinds. In the course of the two years succeeding their introduction, upwards of 50,000 Paragon Umbrellas mere sold.

"Nor was the progress of the Alpaca Umbrella less cheering. Though the material is in some respects inferior to silk, it has been found to wear so much longer, and to cost so much less, that its use is now becoming general among that numerous class with whom economy and an Umbrella are equally indispensable. The sale of Alpaca Umbrellas, in the year 1854, amounted to upwards of 45,000."

Since this time W. & J. S. have sold, under their patent, Umbrellas to the number of nearly four millions.

These facts we will leave to our readers to draw their own inference from; but the very kind reception which the Alpaca Umbrellas have hitherto received, justifies us in asserting, that no material has yet been brought forward which has so thoroughly fulfilled the required conditions. The weight of the Umbrella has also been diminished, and, last not least, the price has decreased in a corresponding ratio. This latter fact is of the very greatest importance, when we remember the immense quantity of Parasols and Umbrellas manufactured during the year in London, and estimated at the enormous value of 500,000 Pounds. In addition, a very great number are made in Manchester and Birmingham.

To those who wish to keep their Umbrellas safe and sound, we may commend the following extract from Cassell's *Household Guide*: —

"Umbrellas are articles which generally suffer more from careless treatment than from legitimate wear and tear; an Umbrella, when properly treated, will last twice as long as one that is not so used. When wet, an Umbrella should neither be distended to dry, which will strain the ribs and covering, and prevent its ever afterwards folding up neatly, nor at once rolled and tied up, which would tend to rust the frame and rot the textile fabric; neither should it, if of silk, be carelessly thrust into an Umbrella-stand, nor allowed to rest against a wall, which would probably discolour, and certainly crease the silk injuriously. It should be shut, but not tied up, and hung from the handle, with the point downwards, till it is nearly, but not quite dry. It should then be neatly and carefully rolled up and tied. In walking with an Umbrella, the hands should be confined to the handle, and not allowed to grasp the silk; otherwise that portion which is held will become greased and discoloured, and the material will be frayed out round the tips, which are points where there is always much stress, and where if will always have a tendency to give way. When not in use, the Umbrella should be protected from dust and injury of any kind by its silk or oilcloth case. When dirty, alpaca umbrellas are best cleaned with a clothes-brush; but brushing is useless for those of silk. Ordinary dirt may be removed from a silk umbrella by means of a clean sponge and cold water, or if the soil should be so tenacious that this will not remove it, a piece of linen rag, dipped in spirits of wine or unsweetened gin, will generally effect the desired end."

Having thus given our readers all the information on the subject in our power; even down to the last quoted paragraph, which may teach them how to preserve their Umbrellas, we may wish them a hearty farewell, hoping they may—long live to use these promoters of comfort and of health, and that they may always be as well shielded by fate from the metaphorical tempests of life, as they are from its physical storms by a good modern Umbrella.

FINIS